KEEPERS AT HOME

Gluten-Free
COOKING

Foods for people with gluten allergies from Keepers At Home kitchens

Front cover: Jelly Roll (page 88) by Nicole Hiebert

1st printing September 2009 5M
2nd printing May 2010 5M
3rd printing November 2010 5M

ISBN-10 digit: 1-933753-11-0
ISBN-13 digit: 978-1-933753-11-9
Design and text: Amy Wengerd, Leah Wengerd
Cover Design: Abigail Troyer
Cover photo: Jason Weaver
Printing: Carlisle Printing

Carlisle Press
WALNUT CREEK

2673 Township Road 421
Sugarcreek, OH 44681

For a free catalog of all Carlisle books call 1.800.852.4482

Thank You!

A special thank-you to *Keepers at Home* readers who have made this book possible. Thank you for sharing your experiences and your favorite foods found here in *Gluten-Free Cooking*. We trust your efforts will be rewarded when others who have gluten allergics enjoy what you so generously contributed here.

Marvin & Miriam Wengerd
Gluten-Free Cooking Editors

Preface

I was three years old when I last ate anything with gluten in it. That was over 20 years ago. After I was diagnosed with Celiac disease in 1988, our lifestyle radically (and permanently!) changed. Celiac disease is a permanent, hereditary disease which renders one completely intolerant to gluten. With gluten found in the majority of our North American diet, this change to a gluten-free diet is not without its challenges, but with this cookbook in your hands you will be far better equipped to handle the adjustment.

When I was first diagnosed, the available options for the would-be gluten-free cook (and more so for the unfortunate eater!) were anything but encouraging. One wasn't sure if the cookies were *supposed* to taste like sawdust, and chances were ten to one you would have to eat your cake with a spoon simply because it would sift through the tines of your fork before it reached your mouth. Those were the days!

But such an experience will not be yours! Recent studies and experiments in the gluten-free field are turning out more and more satisfactory results, to the point now where many non-gluten-free people are shocked to find the desserts they are sampling do not have a single trace of wheat flour in them! Special gums and combinations of various gluten-free flours have turned baking (and eating!) into a scrumptious joy, instead of a burden necessary for survival.

Whether you are new to the field of gluten-free baking (and eating) or a veteran, you will find this cookbook a helpful tool and reliable guide in your kitchen—and a winner in the dining room!

Nicole Hiebert
Worsley, Alberta
July 2009

5

About Keepers at Home Magazine

Started in 1993, Keepers at Home has a mission to encourage women in their God-given calling of being mother and homemakers. Our banner verses were and still are Titus 2:4-5. Speaking to women, Paul encourages, "That they may teach the young women to be sober, to love their husbands, to love their children, to be discreet, chaste, keepers at home, good, obedient to their husbands, that the Word of God be not blasphemed. Four times a year we seek to bless and encourage close to sixteen thousand readers across the world with homemaking articles, recipes, gardening topics, homemade creations and spiritual nourishment all written by our readers and editors.

We live "down the hill" from Walnut Creek, Ohio, a little town famous for its Amish kitchen cooking and other tourist amenities. We invite you to stop by our house if your travels bring you by!

Marvin & Miriam Wengerd family

Amy (Josh), Leah, Rosetta, Emily, David, Lisa, Heidi, Carrie & Jonathan

Ben Jr. & Mary K Troyer family

Jolene (Conrad), Jessica (Charles), Bethany (Daniel) Vonda, Ben Lindan, Justin & Josiah (in heaven)

Table of Contents

Gluten-Free Getting Started

Helping You Get Started

Recently I was in a health food store when I over-
heard a man at the checkout counter who was
buying gluten-free products because he had been diagnosed
with Celiac disease within the last few months. I went up to
him and greeted him with the words, "Join the crowd!"

A tired smile crossed his face. He was thin and you
could see that he was still recovering from the effects of poor
health. "Seems like it's getting to be a bigger crowd all the
time!" he admitted.

That's true. Just a decade ago, most people gave me
a strange look when I told them that I was intolerant to
gluten. Many didn't know what gluten was.

The scene is dramatically different now. On two occasions in the last year I have entered a fast-food restaurant
(out of necessity, I assure you!) and mentally steeled myself
for the stressful ordeal before me—that of explaining my
food restrictions to the staff and asking for a hamburger
patty without a bun. However, on both of these occasions, I
was in for a surprise.

"Oh, you mean Celiac disease?" the first manager asked.
"My best friend has it. Don't worry—my patties and fries are
gluten-free."

"Oh, yes, I understand," the second manager assured us,
"my mother is a Celiac. Let me help you with your menu."

Gluten-intolerance seems to be on the rise. More and
more people are turning to a gluten-free diet in attempt
to clear up digestive problems, fatigue, and/or emotional
and mental difficulties. In many cases, it *is* the answer. For
some, they can do very well if they merely avoid wheat, but
they can still use other gluten grains such as barley, spelt, or
rye. For the true gluten-intolerant person, which definitely
includes Celiacs, even these grains are damaging and unsafe.

At one point, the field was very narrow and bleak for gluten-intolerant people. But today with a wide variety of "safe" grains and gums, we are not deprived at all!

I was diagnosed as a Celiac at the age of three after three months of tests. In those early days, my mother cooked separately for me, and so we always had to have two pots of pasta, two kinds of bread, two toasters, etc. Now our whole family eats gluten-free for the most part. As the years passed, my other sisters began exhibiting adverse reactions to gluten in different ways. One sister had a low immunity and wasn't growing properly. After being put on a gluten-free diet, she started gaining weight and there was a marked improvement in her immunity. Another sister's problems with potty training cleared up. Mysterious stomach aches vanished. Energy levels increased.

The challenge remains to *read each and every label very diligently*. Gluten hides under a score of disguises. You will only occasionally find "gluten" in an ingredient list. Most likely, though, you will find some of the following: modified food starch, hydrolyzed vegetable protein (HVP), hydrolyzed plant protein (HPP), malt extract, malt flavoring, and malt syrup. The first three mentioned may or may not be gluten-free––it depends entirely on whether the starch or protein is derived from wheat or not. Very sensitive people may be wiser to avoid them unless the label specifically states it is derived from a non-gluten source. Personally, I have had very negative effects from modified food starch, so I have chosen to keep away from anything with that ingredient. Malt extract, malt flavoring, and malt syrup are usually extracted from barley. *However, do not confuse this with malt sugar and malt vinegar.* Malt sugar (Maltose) and malt vinegar are both gluten-free.

If you are new to the field of gluten-free cooking/eating, rest assured that the process will soon become second nature. With the increase and improvement of recipes and aware-

11

ness, the path is much easier—and more fun than it used to be. Our family learned long ago that my Celiac disease was a blessing in disguise. It began our journey to better health. May your gluten-free experiences be just as rewarding!

Gluten-Free Flour

There are three ingredients used in my recipes which may or may not already be in your pantry:

Brown rice flour

Tapioca

Xanthan gum

Although xanthan gum can be expensive, it is the key ingredient in gluten-free baking.

Other gluten-free flours include bean flours, buckwheat flour, corn flour, nut flours, potato flour and potato starch flour (the two are different—don't confuse them!), sorghum flour, soy flour, amaranth, quinoa, and millet.

Recent studies have shown that oats may safely be used by most Celiacs. However, they are processed with the same equipment as gluten grains, therefore there is a risk of contamination. Some people are not affected by this, but for those who are really sensitive, pure, uncontaminated oats are available, and should be consumed in limited amounts.

Flours to AVOID include spelt, kamut, club, durum, bulgur, einkorn, semolina, triticale, rye, and barley. These all include at least a trace amount of gluten.

—Nicole Hiebert

Gluten-Free—Our Experience

We discovered our firstborn, a son, had food sensitivities within days of his birth. Dairy products were the biggest culprit, and if I consumed even the smallest amount in a dish, it would affect him. Within a short time after feeding he would wail and cry in pain for up to a half hour at a time. I got tested for food allergies, and eliminated a lot of foods! At nearly one year of age, our son continued to sleep fitfully, thrashing around in his crib. Finally, I removed all gluten from his and my meals. The next day he slept peacefully, and to this day (he's seven now) he gets out of control within hours of consuming gluten products, and he screams out in his sleep.

Living on a gluten-free diet requires constant vigilance. I was a health-conscious cook before, but our special diet has encouraged me to be even more aware of nutrition. GF flour mixes usually consist of starchy products like cornstarch, tapioca starch, etc. I ask myself, "How much nutrition is there in that?" Breads consisting of large quantities of cornstarch are not my idea of a nutritious food that I want my son to consume. Instead, we use corn tortillas a lot. I purchase locally made tortillas by the case and store them in the freezer. We warm them up in our toaster oven just before use.

I make Quick Cornmeal Mush (cornmeal pancakes), GF biscuits or GF cornbread to eat with soups and casseroles. Sometimes we have brown rice cakes or pancakes in place of bread.

I try to always have cooked brown rice or cooked millet in the fridge (I soak the cereals/grains overnight before cooking). Our favorite rice is short-grain organic brown. It has a naturally sweet flavor and is delicious plain when still warm or before it's refrigerated. Instead of baked goods for snacks, we have cold cooked cereal with goat's milk or fruit shake, sliced or dried fruit (bananas, apples, raisins) and nuts and seeds (soaked and dehydrated sunflower seeds, walnuts, etc.).

The cooked rice and millet are also convenient to add to soups, bean dishes, etc. to make them more filling.

Purchasing specialty foods in small bags at the health food store can be very expensive. Instead, I have located sources to purchase organic brown rice, organic millet, organic grains, Celtic sea salt, etc. in bulk at a fraction of the cost.

We freeze huge quantities of fresh fruits in season to use for fruit shakes/smoothies. We also dehydrate fruits for winter snacking, and grow and freeze vegetables to enjoy later. I leave our peas raw (unblanched) to freeze and thaw them by letting warm water run over them just before serving. Delicious in salads or with pasta dishes, casseroles, etc. We prefer this over cooked peas. These different methods ensure that we eat plenty of raw foods without the high cost of buying fresh produce during the winter.

Of course, I still buy some fresh fruits like oranges and grapefruits and some greens like celery and coleslaw.

Making everything from scratch is time-consuming but a requirement to stick to gluten-free foods. It also involves a lot of canning. I make all my own relish, tomato soup, vegetable soups, etc. In a way this is a real blessing because homegrown and homemade is much more nutritious and chemical-free than purchased foods.

We eat simply, but our meals are generally nutritious and delicious. Our son really appreciates food and often cheers when he sees what is being served. He has many favorite meals.

God can turn our trials into blessings, and I feel that's what He has done with our gluten-free, sugar-free, dairy-free diet. I still wish we could eat whole grains, but in the meantime we are thankful to live in a land of plenty where we can eat lots of nourishing food.

—David & Susie Wiebe, Manitou, MB

Changing Recipes to Gluten-Free

Here are several suggestions for changing wheat recipes to gluten-free:

Some baked goods work fine with only rice flour, but many get better using the gluten-free mix. I almost always use the mix for cookies and bars.

Adding an extra egg often improves the product as rice flour is lower in protein.

Add 1 tsp. gelatin to approximately 3 cups flour in cookie recipes.

Adding xanthan gum is important. Use in the following amounts:

for breads: ¾ tsp. per cup of flour

for cakes: ½ tsp. per cup of flour

for cookies: ¼-½ tsp. per cup of flour

—Donna Lois Wadel

Tips for Baking with Gluten-Free Flours

Rice flour has a grainy texture. It can be made smoother by blending it with the liquids in the recipe, bringing the mixture to a boil, then cooling it before adding the other ingredients.

Gluten-free flours produce a dry texture in cakes. Moisture can be preserved by icing or storing the cake in a tightly covered container.

Baked goods prepared from rice and soy flour require a longer baking time and lower temperature than conventional preparation.

Muffins and biscuits made of rice flour have a better texture if they are baked in small sizes.

Gluten-free baked products rise better if the leavening agent is dissolved in the liquid before being added to the other ingredients. Also, the amount of leavening agent should be greatly increased to make a lighter texture when using heavy flours.

For 1 tablespoon wheat flour, substitute:
1½ teaspoons cornstarch
1½ teaspoons potato starch
1½ teaspoons arrowroot starch
1½ teaspoons rice flour
2 teaspoons quick-cooking tapioca

For 1 cup wheat flour, substitute:
1 cup corn flour
¾ cup plain cornmeal, coarse
1 scant cup plain cornmeal, fine
⅝ cup potato flour
¾ cup rice flour
1⅓ cups ground rolled oats

Breads and baked products made without the benefit of gluten lack elasticity, good volume, and a light, even texture. Flours commonly substituted for wheat flour include potato starch flour, rice flour, soy flour, tapioca flour, cornstarch, cornmeal, corn flour, and sometimes buckwheat. None of these makes a "real" loaf of bread, but breads and baked goods made from gluten-free flours are just as delicious.

Potato starch is a very fine white flour. It works well as a thickening agent and may be used successfully in baking, especially in products such as sponge cakes where eggs supply the needed structure. Recipes using one cup all-purpose wheat flour can be adjusted by substituting ⅝ cup potato flour. In most baking, it's best to use potato flour in combination with others because of its strong flavor.

Rice flour is made from the broken kernels of milled rice. Its bland flavor and grainy texture when used alone makes it a good choice to combine with potato starch. If used alone, substitute 7/8 cup rice flour for one cup all-purpose flour.

Soy flour is a light, yellow flour with a high protein and fat content and a characteristic "nutty" flavor. It is sometimes used to replace up to two tablespoons per cup of all-purpose white flour in regular baking, as a way to increase the protein content of the baked product.

In spite of its protein enrichment qualities, soy flour does not produce a very desirable product when used as the only flour in a mixture. It is most successfully used in combination with other flours in products containing chocolate, nuts, and spices, where a nutty flavor is desirable.

Corn flour is prepared by grinding white or yellow corn in a process similar to cornmeal, but much finer. Corn flour is different from cornstarch. Cornstarch is the refined starch from the endosperm of corn. Corn flour, combined with equal parts of potato or rice flour, is an excellent substitute for wheat flour. For convenience, sift several cups of the mixture together six times, then store in a cool, dry place and use as needed. For each recipe, use one cup of the mixture per cup of flour called for, and twice the amount of baking powder specified.

Gluten-Free and Diabetes

Dr. Marten from Strasburg (who treats MSUD children among Mennonites) has mentioned that a gluten-free diet can cause diabetes. I asked my doctor about it, and she said there would be a big difference if a person doesn't use the starches (corn, potato, tapioca) and gums (guar and xanthan) in baking. If people buy ready-to-eat gluten-free foods, they are usually loaded with such, so it is much better to make from scratch and try to avoid or cut back as much as possible. It is rather hard to always have good results.

In sourdough baking, recipes that have plenty of liquid are easiest. Half as much liquid as flour is about the limit to use.

In baking with rice, recipes with plenty of eggs turn out better and can actually help to replace the gums.

—No name please

Gluten-Free Flour Mixes

Gluten-Free Flour Mixture
Rebecca Bontreger

2 cups rice flour   ⅔ cup potato starch
⅓ cup tapioca starch   1 Tbsp. xanthan gum

Mix together well. Use this mixture to exchange cup for cup in the recipes calling for flour (gluten).

Gluten-Free Flour Mix
Nicole Hiebert

6 cups brown rice flour   3 cups tapioca starch

Sift together and store in a dry, dark place. Transform your favorite recipes into gluten-free by:

—using cup for cup in exchange for regular flour
—adding ½ tsp. of xanthan gum per one cup of flour
—adding an extra egg *if eggs are already in the recipe*

Voila! Gluten-free becomes easy!

Original GF Flour Mix
Mrs. Esther Beachy

2 cups rice flour   ⅔ cup potato starch flour
⅓ cup tapioca flour

This can be used cup for cup in exchange for regular flour.

GF Flour Mix 2
Mrs. Esther Beachy

3 cups rice flour   3 cups tapioca flour
3 cups cornstarch   3 Tbsp. potato flour

This can be used cup for cup in exchange for regular flour.

GF Flour Blend
Mrs. John (Emma) Mullet

2 cups potato flour   1 cup tapioca flour
6 cups rice flour

Mix together and store in airtight container. Substitute for flour in your favorite recipe.

Millet Flour Mix
Mrs. Lawrence Nolt

6 cups millet flour   4 cups tapioca flour
2 cups cornstarch

This is the mix I use for all my husband's gluten-free baking. I just use it in place of regular flour, then add ½-1 tsp. xanthan gum per cup of flour, as a binder. Otherwise some things will just fall apart.

Gluten-Free Flour
Mrs. Larry (Liana) Cable

3 cups tapioca starch   6 cups potato starch
18 cups rice flour

Mix well. Add 1 tsp. xanthan gum per 2 cups gluten-free flour.

Gluten-Free Mix
Donna Lois Wadel

2 parts brown rice flour   ⅓ part tapioca flour
⅔ part potato starch flour

Mix well and use cup for cup to replace wheat flour.

Gluten-Free Flour Mixture
Mrs. Jayne Martin

6 cups rice flour   1 cup tapioca flour
2 cups potato starch   4½ tsp. xanthan gum

Mix together thoroughly and use cup for cup in any re except yeast baking.

my gluten-free notes

_____

_____

_____

_____

_____

_____

_____

_____

_____

_____

_____

_____

_____

_____

_____

_____

_____

_____

_____

_____

_____

Gluten-Free
Yeast Breads

Favorite Gluten-Free Bread   Mrs. Thomas Beachy

Dry ingredients:

2 cups brown rice flour	1 Tbsp. xanthan gum
½ cup potato starch	1½ tsp. salt
½ cup tapioca flour	1 Tbsp. active dry yeast
⅓ cup cornstarch	

Liquids:

3 eggs	1 tsp. cider vinegar
1 Tbsp. honey	1¼ cups milk
4 Tbsp. canola oil	

Measure all dry ingredients in medium bowl. Stir or whisk well. Combine liquids and mix well. Large bread machine method: Transfer wet and dry ingredients and yeast to baking pan of bread machine in the order suggested by the manufacturer. Press start. Help mix dough during kneading cycle. Mixture will be very thick. Use one rise and one knead cycle if machine is programmable. Remove upon completion of baking cycle. Oven method: Preheat oven to 375°. Lightly oil a 9 x 5" loaf pan. Add yeast to mix and beat in liquids. Beat two minutes. Scrape into loaf pan. Cover with plastic wrap and let rise to top of pan. Bake 40-45 minutes or until lightly browned. Cool on wire rack before slicing.

Rice Bread for Bread Machine   Mrs. Jayne Martin

1¾ cups water	1 tsp. salt
2 Tbsp. butter	3½ cups rice flour mixture*
2 Tbsp. sugar	1½ tsp. yeast

Put into bread machine in order given and set on basic cycle.
*See Jayne Martin's Gluten-Free Flour Mixture recipe on page 21.

GF "Wheat" Bread

Mrs. Rebecca Bontreger

¼ cup olive oil	4 well beaten eggs
¼ cup honey	½ cup warm water
1 Tbsp. lemon juice	2 tsp. sugar
1 Tbsp. vinegar	4 tsp. yeast
1 Tbsp. lecithin	2 cups tapioca starch
1½ tsp. salt	2 cups brown rice flour
1½ cup boiling water	⅔ cup Dari-Free* powdered milk
½ cup buckwheat flour (opt.)	4 tsp. xanthan gum

Combine first nine ingredients in order given. Next put yeast and sugar in warm water. Set aside. In another bowl, mix last four ingredients together well. Pour half of this flour mixture into first bowl with nine ingredients. Stir well. Pour yeast mixture in next. Stir well. Pour last half of flour mixture in. Stir well again. Dough will be more like cake batter. Do not add more flour or mix with hands. Let rise once or twice, stirring down each time. Spoon into smaller bread pans. (If you use 3 bread pans, bake for 40-45 minutes. If you use 4-5 small pans, bake for 30-35 minutes.) Let rise before baking but not till double. If you make three loaves, sprinkle tapioca starch over loaves before baking to prevent excessive browning. Bake in hot oven—375-400°. Do not take out till bottom comes out and is browned and time is up. Cool completely wrapped in towel with loaves lying on side before slicing. Reheat any day-old bread by steaming, or make toast with butter. Very good!

*Dari-Free can be obtained from Vance's Foods, 1.800.497.4834.

True Yeast Bread

Mrs. Thomas Beachy

3 cups GF flour mix*   ½ cup lukewarm water
¼ cup sugar   1½ Tbsp. yeast
3½ tsp. xanthan gum   ¼ cup butter
⅔ cup dry milk powder   1¼ cups water
1½ tsp. salt   1 tsp. vinegar
2 tsp. sugar   3 eggs

Combine flour, sugar, xanthan gum, milk powder, and salt in bowl of heavy-duty mixer. Dissolve the two tsp. of sugar in the half cup of lukewarm water and mix in the yeast. Set aside while you combine the butter and water in saucepan and heat until butter melts. Turn mixer on low. Blend dry ingredients and slowly add butter, water mixture and vinegar. Blend, then add eggs. This mixture should feel slightly warm. Pour the yeast mixture into the ingredients in the bowl and beat at highest speed for two minutes. Place mixing bowl in a warm place, cover with plastic wrap and a towel, and let the dough rise approximately 1-1½ hours or until doubled. Return to mixer and beat on high for three minutes. Spoon the dough into three small (2.5 x 5") greased loaf pans or one large one. Use muffin tins and bake any remainder as small rolls. Or make all rolls (approximately 18).

* GF flour mix for above recipe: 2 cups brown rice flour, ⅔ cup potato starch flour, ⅓ cup tapioca flour

Old-Fashioned Potato Bread
Nicole Hiebert

Dry ingredients:

3 cups GF Flour Mix*	1 tsp. unflavored Knox gelatin
2½ tsp. xanthan gum	3 tsp. instant yeast
1½ tsp. salt	

Wet ingredients:

2 eggs	1 tsp. vinegar
3 Tbsp. oil	3 Tbsp. honey

Mix together the dry ingredients in a medium bowl. In a larger bowl, beat the wet ingredients. Then add to the wet: 1 medium potato, peeled and grated (loose ¼-½ cup), and beat. Then add to the wet: 1¼ cups warm water. Using beaters on low, gradually add dry to wet. Beat on highest speed for 3½ minutes. Scrape into two small bread pans, well greased, or into one large one. Cover and let rise just to top of pan. Bake in 350° oven. Bake small loaves for 45 minutes - cover with aluminum foil after the first 15 minutes. Bake the large loaf for 65 minutes— cover with foil after first 25 minutes in oven. *See Nicole Hiebert's GF Flour Mix recipe on page 20.

No-Gluten Bread *(bread machine version)* Serena Yoder

1¾ cup buttermilk   1 tsp. vinegar
4 egg whites

Mix together the above three ingredients and pour into the bread machine. Put all of the following seven ingredients together in a bowl and mix well. Then add the mixture to the liquid in the bread machine.

2 cups brown rice flour   salt to taste, opt.
1¼ cup tapioca flour   4½ tsp. active dry yeast
1½ tsp. dark brown sugar   ⅓ cup ground flaxseed
3½ tsp. xanthan gum

Place the ingredients in your bread machine pan in the order directed by the manufacturer. Some machines call for liquids first, others call for liquids last. Use the machine's rapid-bake setting. Watch the mixing during the first five minutes. Scrape down the sides of pan with a rubber spatula to insure good mixing. Mix thoroughly with the spatula as it's quite sticky but will bake okay.

No-Gluten Bread *(by hand)*   Serena Yoder

1¾ cup buttermilk (or use rice, soy, or potato)
1 tsp. vinegar (or 2 Tbsp. lemon juice if using non-dairy)
4 eggs

Put eggs in Kitchen Aid mixing bowl. Beat well. Warm buttermilk to 110°. Add to the eggs. Also add vinegar or lemon juice to the eggs and mix well. Put all of the following ingredients in a bowl, mix well, then add to the liquid in the Kitchen Aid bowl.

2 cups brown rice flour	salt to taste, opt.
1¼ cup tapioca flour	4½ tsp. active dry yeast
1½ tsp. dark brown sugar	⅓ cup ground flaxseed
3½ tsp. xanthan gum	

Mix slightly (till flour is mixed) then put Kitchen Aid on top speed and beat 3 minutes and 30 seconds. Grease a 10 x 5¼ x 3" glass pan or two 8.5 x 4.5 x 2.5" pans. Lightly flour bottom of pan(s). Spoon dough into pan. With a wet spatula, smooth top of dough. Let dough rise till it reaches the top of pan. Bake at 350° for one hour.

Tips: Unbaked dough should be consistency of soft mashed potatoes. If bread "falls" after it's baked then decrease the liquid 1 Tbsp. each time till bread turns out right. This is a heavy and sticky type bread. Nuts, cinnamon, and raisins can be added to dry mixture to make different kinds of non-gluten bread.

Gluten-Free Bread
Mrs. Thomas Beachy

1 cup warm water
2 Tbsp. honey
2¼ tsp. yeast
2¼ cups flour blend*
⅓ cup dry milk powder
2 tsp. xanthan gum

1 tsp. salt
¼ tsp. soy lecithin granules
2 large eggs
3 Tbsp. olive oil or melted butter
1 tsp. vinegar

Add honey and yeast to warm water, let dissolve. Mix dry ingredients, then add liquids and eggs. Beat for two minutes on high speed. Spoon into a greased 9 x 5 x 2" pan and let rise to top of pan. Bake at 300° for 45-50 minutes.
*See recipe below.

Gluten-Free Flour Blend
Mrs. Thomas Beachy

1½ cups sorghum flour
1½ cups potato starch

1 cup tapioca flour
½ cup corn flour (not cornmeal)

These items are available from: Bob's Red Mill, 5209 SE International Way, Milwaukie, OR 97222 or call: 1.800.349.2173. Call and ask for a free catalog. It's very informative on gluten-free flours and mixes.

Rice Bread

Laura Miller

Dissolve in small bowl:

2 tsp. honey   ½ cup warm water

Sprinkle into warm water, then set aside for 10 minutes:

1 Tbsp. active dry yeast

Mix well: (if using animal fat, heat to melt, then cool to luke-warm)

1⁴/₅ cups water   ¼ cup honey

¼ cup oil

Combine in mixing bowl:

1 cup brown rice flour   3½ tsp. xanthan gum

2 cups white rice flour   1½ tsp. salt

Combine all liquids, mix well.

2 large eggs, or egg substitute

Beat eggs well, combine with liquids. Add liquids to dry mixture, mix at highest speed of mixer for two minutes. Pour dough into greased bowl. Let rise in warm place until doubled, approximately 1-1½ hours. Return to mixing bowl. Beat three minutes. Pour dough in two small or one large greased loaf pan. Let rise until dough is slightly above top of pan. Bake at 400° for 10 minutes. Place foil over bread and bake 50 minutes more. I bake mine at 350° for 55 minutes for two small loaves. Best bread I've tasted so far.

NOTE: Measure ingredients *very* carefully. The dough looks like cookie dough, but don't be alarmed. Bread structure is better if baked in 2 small loaf pans.

Sourdough Rice Bread

Mabel Zimmerman

12-24 hours before baking, mix the following:

3 cups brown rice flour	1½ cups sweet rice flour
2½ cups kefir or yogurt*	

Soak in a glass bowl or other glass container in a warm place with a plate or plastic wrap on top. When ready to mix bread, beat for 5-10 minutes:

8 large eggs

To the sourdough, mix the following in while it's warm:

3 Tbsp. coconut oil OR
  4 Tbsp. olive oil

Stir in the remaining ingredients:

½ cup flaxseed, ground	2 tsp. salt
½ cup coconut flour	¼ cup apple juice concentrate
2 tsp. baking soda	½ cup cooked pumpkin

Fold sourdough mixture into beaten eggs just until thoroughly mixed. Pour into two small greased loaf pans. Bake at 350° for 45 minutes or longer. (Check with toothpick before removing from oven.) Let cool 15 minutes before removing from pans. Cool completely before slicing, then freeze what isn't used the same day, as it gets dry quickly. *If dairy-free, use 4 Tbsp. vinegar or lemon juice, and add water to make 2½ cups.

NOTES: This is a heavy, moist bread. Experiment until it's like you want it. It could be improved by adding tapioca, potato, and/or cornstarch for part of the flour or the gums (guar or xanthan), but we choose to avoid those high-carbohydrate ingredients. The flaxseed and coconut flour give this excellent fiber. Coconut flour is exceptionally high in fiber and can be purchased in some health food stores. Two known brands are Tropical Traditions and Bob's Red Mill. Apple juice improves the flavor and gives it some sweetness. Sweet rice is more glutenous than other rice, and gives more moisture, as also does the pumpkin.

Gluten-Free

Quick Breads

Zucchini Bread

Nicole Hiebert

Dry ingredients:

3 cups GF Flour Mix*	1½ tsp. baking powder
1½ tsp. xanthan gum	2 tsp. cinnamon
1 tsp. salt	1 cup chopped nuts
1½ tsp. baking soda	

Wet ingredients:

4 eggs	⅔ cup oil
4 cups shredded zucchini	2 tsp. vanilla
1 cup honey	

Combine dry ingredients in a bowl. In a large bowl, beat eggs well with a whisk until frothy. Add remaining wet ingredients and the dry, and mix well with a spoon. Bake at 325° for 1 hour in 2 greased loaf pans. *See Nicole Hiebert's GF Flour Mix recipe on page 20.

Rice Bread

Mrs. Elvin Zimmerman

Dissolve:

½ tsp. baking soda in:	1 cup apple juice or water

Set aside. In a mixer bowl combine:

2 beaten eggs	2 Tbsp. olive oil
2 cups brown rice flour	½ tsp. salt
2 tsp. baking powder	

Add soda liquid. Mix until just moistened. Pour into greased loaf pan.

Yeast-Free Brown Rice Bread   Nicole Hiebert

Beat with whisk:

4 eggs

Add and mix well:

2 cups soy milk   4 Tbsp. honey

4 Tbsp. oil

Sift together:

5 cups brown rice flour   1 tsp. salt

½ cup tapioca flour   ½ tsp. allspice (opt.)

2 tsp. cream of tartar   3 tsp. xanthan gum

2 tsp. baking soda

Slowly add dry to wet, beating with spoon or whisk. Pour into well greased bread pans (2 or 3). Bake at 350° for 45-50 minutes.

Gluten-Free Corn Bread 1   Mrs. Thomas Beachy

2 eggs, well beaten   1 Tbsp. baking powder

⅓ cup olive oil   1 Tbsp. vanilla

⅛ cup raw sugar or honey   1½ cups cornmeal

1½ cup sour milk   1½ cups rice flour

½ tsp. baking soda   ½ tsp. stevia powder

Beat eggs hard until thick and fluffy. Add rest of ingredients without beating. Stevia may be mixed a bit into the flour before adding. When all ingredients are added, stir well with spoon. Pour into a greased 9 x 13" pan. Bake at 400° for 30-35 minutes.

Gluten-Free Corn Bread 2 Susie Wiebe

Combine in medium bowl:

½ cup cornmeal	½ tsp. baking soda
½ cup rice flour or GF flour	1 tsp. cream of tartar
1 tsp. xanthan gum	¼ tsp. fine Celtic sea salt

Add:

1 egg (beaten with fork)	1½ tsp. melted honey
½ cup sour cream or water	

Stir briefly, then add:

2 Tbsp. melted butter

Stir just to combine. Spread in greased or parchment paper lined 8 x 8" pan. Bake at 350° for 15 minutes. Can also be baked in muffin tins. Mini-muffins are a treat. Double recipe for a 9 x 13" pan. Delicious with soup or bean dishes.

Gluten-Free Corn Bread 3 Mrs. Elizabeth Beachy

1½ cup cornmeal	5 tsp. baking powder
1 cup rice flour	6 Tbsp. lard or olive oil
½ cup cornstarch	3 eggs
¾ tsp. salt	1¾ cup water
1 tsp. guar gum	

Stir all ingredients together. If using lard you can decrease the amount by ¾. Guar gum is for texture but is said to be unhealthy. The batter will seem rather thin. Bake at 350° till done.

Buttery Corn Bread

Nicole Hiebert

Dry ingredients:

2⅓ cups GF Flour Mix*	4½ tsp. baking powder
2 tsp. xanthan gum	1 tsp. salt
1 cup cornmeal	

Wet ingredients:

⅔ cup butter, softened	4 eggs
½ cup honey	1⅔ cup milk

Cream butter and honey in a large mixing bowl. Combine eggs and milk in separate bowl. Combine dry ingredients in a third bowl. Add dry to butter and honey alternately with egg mixture. Pour into a greased 13 x 9 x 2" baking pan. Bake at 400° for 20-30 minutes or until a toothpick inserted near the center comes out clean. Cut into squares and serve warm. *See Nicole Hiebert's GF Flour Mix recipe on page 20.

Bread Without Yeast

Mrs. Jayne Martin

2 cups water	3½ cups gluten-free flour
2 Tbsp. lard or butter	2 Tbsp. baking powder
2 Tbsp. sugar	

I use a millet flour mixture (same as rice), so baking time may vary with flours. Mix together and put in 8.5 x 4.5 x 2.5" bread pan. Put foil over top and bake at least one hour at 350°. It is very crumbly, but good sliced when cold and then toasted crisp, which helps keep it together.

Sourdough Rice Bread

Mabel Zimmerman

7-24 hours before baking bread, mix:

3½ cups brown rice flour   2½ cups kefir or yogurt
1 cup sweet brown rice flour

Soak in a glass bowl or container in a warm place with a plate or plastic wrap over top. When ready to do the rest of the mixing, beat for 5-10 minutes at high speed:

8 large eggs

Meanwhile, add the rest of the ingredients to the sourdough and mix slightly:

¼ cup frozen apple juice   ½ cup ground flaxseeds
   concentrate   1 cup coconut flour
½ cup cooked pumpkin   2 tsp. baking soda
¼ cup olive oil   2 tsp. salt

Fold sourdough mixture into beaten eggs with mixer. Pour into two small greased bread pans. Bake at 375° for 45 minutes. Check if done with a toothpick. Let set in pans for 15 minutes before removing.

Gluten-Free Buns

Mrs. Joe Garber

Combine in equal proportions the following flours: rice, millet, corn, buckwheat, sorghum. Mix well:

2 cups flour mix   1 heaping Tbsp. baking powder
½ cup tapioca flour   ½ tsp. salt

Add:

⅓ cup oil   ½ cup applesauce
1 cup water or milk

Stir till just mixed. Fry on greased hot skillet. They are more fluffy if a lid is on the pan while baking.

Gluten-Free

Muffins

Corn Bread Muffins
Mrs. Rebecca Bontreger

2 eggs, well beaten
½ cup rice milk
4 Tbsp. olive oil
1 cup cornmeal
½ cup brown rice flour

½ cup tapioca starch
2 Tbsp. sugar
4 tsp. baking powder
1 tsp. salt

Mix wet ingredients. Mix dry ingredients. Mix together well. Bake in mini muffin tins at 375-400° until done.

Pumpkin-Almond Muffins
Ina Schrock

1 cup rice flour
¾ cup ground almonds
½ tsp. baking powder
1 tsp. baking soda
½ tsp. salt
½ tsp. cinnamon
⅛ tsp. cloves
⅛ tsp. nutmeg

½ tsp. ginger
1 tsp. stevia
¼ cup butter
2 eggs
1 cup pumpkin
⅓ cup soy milk
½ cup raisins

Preheat oven to 350°. Line a muffin pan. In a large bowl, mix dry ingredients. In a separate bowl, beat butter and eggs till very light. Add pumpkin and stevia and beat again. Add dry ingredients alternately with soy milk. Add raisins. Pour into muffin tins and bake about 30 minutes or till toothpick comes out clean. Makes 12 muffins.

Blueberry Muffins

Mrs. Larry (Liana) Cable

2⅓ cups gluten-free flour
1 tsp. unflavored gelatin
1 tsp. xanthan gum
2½ tsp. baking powder
⅔ cup Sucanat (or ⅓ c. honey)
1 tsp. salt

1 cup dairy-free milk
¼ cup olive oil
2 large eggs
1 tsp. vanilla
2 tsp. grated lemon peel
2 cups blueberries

Glaze:

2 Tbsp. honey

4 Tbsp. lemon juice

Mix dry ingredients together. Mix wet ingredients together. Combine the wet and dry ingredients. Stir until mixed well. Fold in blueberries. Spoon into muffin tins. Bake at 400° for 20 minutes. Remove from oven. Combine glaze ingredients. Spoon over muffins.

Plain Muffins

Nicole Hiebert

Dry ingredients:

2 cups GF Flour Mix*
1 tsp. xanthan gum

3½ tsp. baking powder
½ tsp. salt

Wet ingredients:

2 eggs
1 cup milk

⅛ cup honey
¼ cup oil

Stir together dry ingredients in a large bowl. In a small bowl, beat together the wet ingredients. Add wet to dry and stir well. Fill greased muffin cups and bake at 400° for 12-15 minutes or until golden brown. Variations: For Blueberry Muffins, add one cup fresh blueberries or quick-frozen blueberries to dry. Flour berries thoroughly by tossing them through the dry. Then add wet. For Spice Muffins, increase honey slightly and sift in 1 tsp. cinnamon, ½ tsp. nutmeg, and ½ tsp. allspice into dry. *See Nicole Hiebert's GF Flour Mix recipe on page 20.

Morning Glory Muffins

Nicole Hiebert

Dry ingredients:

2 cups GF Flour Mix*	2 cups grated carrot
1 tsp. xanthan gum	½ cup raisins
3 tsp. baking soda	½ cup coconut
2 tsp. cinnamon	1 apple, peeled and grated
½ tsp. salt	

Wet ingredients:

4 eggs (5 if small)	2 tsp. vanilla
1 cup oil	½-1 cup honey

Mix first five dry ingredients in large bowl. Stir in the other four dry ingredients. In a small bowl, mix the wet ingredients. Stir wet into dry. Fill greased muffin cups almost half full. Bake in 325° oven until done. *See Nicole Hiebert's GF Flour Mix recipe on page 20.

Ginger Muffins

Nicole Hiebert

Dry ingredients:

1¾ cup GF Flour Mix*	½ tsp. cinnamon
1 tsp. xanthan gum	½ tsp. ginger
1 tsp. baking soda	¼ tsp. cloves
¼ tsp. salt	

Wet ingredients:

¼ cup butter	½ cup molasses
⅛ cup honey	¼ cup hot water
2 eggs	¼ cup hot water

In a large bowl, beat together butter, honey, eggs, molasses, and first amount of hot water. Measure dry ingredients into same bowl and stir together. Gradually stir second amount of hot water into batter. Fill greased muffin tins ¾ full. Bake in 400° oven for 20-25 minutes until inserted toothpick comes out clean. Cool in pan 5 minutes, then remove. Makes 12 muffins.

*See Nicole Hiebert's GF Flour Mix recipe on page 20.

Banana Muffins
Nicole Hiebert

Dry ingredients:

1¾ cup GF Flour Mix*	½ tsp. baking powder
1 tsp. xanthan gum	½ tsp. salt
1 tsp. baking soda	

Wet ingredients:

½ cup butter	3 eggs
½ cup honey	1 cup ripe bananas, mashed

Cream butter and honey together. Beat in eggs, one at a time, beating until smooth. Add mashed bananas and blend in. In second bowl, stir dry ingredients. Add to wet and stir well. Fill greased muffin tins and bake in preheated 400° oven for about 18-20 minutes. Variation: For Banana Chip Muffins, add ¾ cup semisweet chocolate chips. *See Nicole Hiebert's GF Flour Mix recipe on page 20.

Gluten-Free Timbits
Mrs. Jayne Martin

Cream:

½ cup butter	2 eggs
1 cup white sugar	

Add:

1¾ cup brown rice flour	1 tsp. nutmeg
2 tsp. gf baking powder	

Complete above. Then combine 1 tsp. baking soda with 1 cup sour cream (water works too) and stir (it will froth slightly) and add to the above mixture. Bake at 350° for 8-10 minutes or until browned. While baking, melt ½-¾ cup butter and combine 1 tsp. cinnamon with ½ cup white sugar. While timbits are still warm, dip in melted butter and roll in sugar/cinnamon mixture. Store in airtight container. This recipe can be used for regular size muffins, slab cake, layer cake, loaf, or mini-muffins. For big cupcakes, just dip the top.

Gluten-Free

Biscuits

Bob's Best Biscuits

2 cups Rita's GF mix (below) 1 tsp. honey
1½ tsp. xanthan gum   2 Tbsp. oil
¾ tsp. salt   1 egg
4 tsp. baking powder   ¾ cup water

Pat into one inch circle. Bake at 425° for 15 minutes.

Rita's Gluten-Free Biscuit Mix

3 cups brown rice flour   2 tsp. xanthan gum
1 cup tapioca flour   1½ cup potato starch
⅔ cup corn flour   1 cup bean flour

GF Biscuits

Mrs. Rebecca Bontreger

2 cups tapioca starch   1 Tbsp. honey
1 Tbsp. baking powder   1 egg, beaten
1 tsp. salt   ½ cup rice milk
4 Tbsp. olive oil

Sift dry ingredients. Beat egg in measuring cup and add wet
ingredients till ⅔-¾ cup liquid. Mix dry and wet ingredients
together well. Bake in mini muffin tins or drop by teaspoon on
cookie sheet. Bake at 400° till golden. Serve while warm.

Kentucky Biscuits
Mrs. Liana Cable

2 tsp. xanthan gum	1 Tbsp. Sucanat (optional)
2 cups gluten-free flour	½ cup butter or olive oil
2½ tsp. baking powder	¾ cup dairy-free milk
½ tsp. baking soda	with 1 Tbsp. lemon juice

Mix dry ingredients in a bowl. Cut in butter. Add milk. Mix quickly to make a soft dough. Turn onto a lightly greased cookie sheet. Roll out into 6 x 6" squares, or to desired thickness. Bake at 400° for 15 minutes. May drop these biscuits, also.

Sky-High Biscuits
Mrs. Liana Cable

2 tsp. xanthan gum	¼ cup butter
3 cups gluten-free flour	½ cup olive oil
4½ tsp. baking powder	1 egg, beaten
1 Tbsp. Sucanat (optional)	1 cup dairy-free milk
¾ tsp. cream of tartar	

Combine flours, baking powder, Sucanat, and cream of tartar. Cut in butter and oil until mixture resembles coarse cornmeal. Add egg and milk, stirring well. Drop onto cookie sheet. Bake at 400° for 15-20 minutes.

Coconut Country Biscuits
Mrs. Thomas Beachy

¾ cup brown rice flour   ¼ tsp. salt
¼ cup coconut flour   ¼ cup butter
2 Tbsp. potato starch   ½ cup buttermilk
1 Tbsp. baking powder

Preheat oven to 450°. Combine dry ingredients. Cut butter into flour mixture until it resembles small peas. Stir in buttermilk to form soft dough. Place mixture on top of wax paper and press to one inch thickness. Cut with 2" biscuit cutter and place on baking sheet. Bake for 10-12 minutes. Yields 9 biscuits.

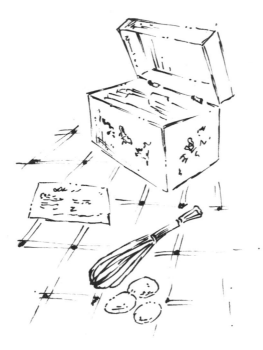

Gluten-Free Breakfast

Gluten-Free Breakfast Cake   The B Sisters

Wet ingredients:

1 cup diced apple	⅔ cup buttermilk
¼ cup pure cane sugar	½ cup molasses
(or honey)	1 tsp. lemon juice
½ cup oil (or melted butter)	2 beaten eggs

Dry ingredients:

2 cups GF baking flour	2 tsp. cinnamon
1 tsp. baking soda	1 tsp. allspice
1 tsp. nutmeg	1 tsp. cloves
1 cup raisins	½ cup chopped nuts

Combine the wet ingredients. In another bowl, combine the dry ingredients. (You can stir the dry ingredients with a whisk to lighten.) Gradually add flour mixture to wet mixture. Stir in nuts and raisins. Pour batter into a greased 9 x 13" pan. When ready to bake, preheat oven to 350°. Bake for 40-50 minutes, or until cake springs back when touched lightly in the center. Serves six.

This is a delicious and simple recipe that we have found very forgiving to changes (such as using gluten-free flours). It can be made the night before, refrigerated, and baked in the morning.

Gluten-Free Waffles   Melinda Hollback

2 eggs, separated	½ cup tapioca flour
1 cup yogurt	1½ tsp. baking soda
¼ cup oil	1 tsp. baking powder
1 cup rice flour	1 Tbsp. vanilla

Mix everything except egg whites together. Beat the egg whites until frothy, fold in. Bake in waffle iron. I have added fruit, cinnamon, etc. to these with great results. I triple the recipe and keep it in a pitcher in the fridge for waffles anytime. Lasts one week.

Ezra's Gluten-Free Pancakes

Susie Wiebe

Combine in large bowl:

2 cups millet flour
¼ cup rice flour
¼ cup rice bran
2 tsp. cream of tartar

2 tsp. baking soda
½ tsp. fine Celtic sea salt
2 tsp. xanthan gum

In 4 cup measuring cup, place:

1½ cups applesauce
1 cup cider*

¼ cup olive oil or melted butter
water* (fill to 4 cup mark)

Stir to combine, then stir into dry ingredients just till moistened. Fry in greased pan or on griddle. Serve with raw applesauce and maple syrup, or honey-sweetened jam, or almond butter and honey, or your favorite toppings. Pancakes are best served warm or rewarmed, but can serve as a bread replacement when cold.

*Cider and water can be replaced with liquid of choice, such as milk, buttermilk, part yogurt, etc.

Cake Pan Pancakes

1 cup GF flour
3 large eggs, beaten

1 cup milk
½ tsp. salt

Put 2 Tbsp. oil and 2 Tbsp. butter in 9 x 13" Pyrex baking dish. Put in oven to melt (375°). Meanwhile stir together other ingredients, then pour onto butter and oil. Bake 20 minutes or till edges are browning. Batter will puff up, then fall after baking. Good with blueberries and maple syrup.

Rice Flour Pancakes
Mrs. Elizabeth Beachy

2 cups rice flour
1 cup Perma-Flo
1 Tbsp. melted butter (or lard, olive oil, coconut oil)
2 cups milk or water

1 egg, slightly beaten
1 tsp. salt

In a bowl stir together dry ingredients. Whisk in milk, egg, and butter. Lightly oil griddle. It needs to be hot. Oil griddle occasionally—not every time. Cook until done, turning once.

GF Pancake Mix
Mrs. Thomas Beachy

3 cups rice flour
1 cup potato flour
7 tsp. baking powder

2 tsp. soda
1 tsp. salt

Mix all together. For pancake batter:

1 cup pancake mix
1 egg, well beaten

¼ cup olive oil
½ cup buttermilk

Mix and fry in hot pan.

Golden Pancakes
Mrs. Rebecca Bontreger

2 eggs, well beaten
⅔ cup rice milk
4 Tbsp. olive oil
¼ cup tapioca starch
1¼ cup brown rice flour

⅓ cup potato starch
¾ tsp. salt
2 tsp. baking powder
¼ tsp. soda
2 Tbsp. sugar

Mix wet ingredients. Put dry ingredients into sifter and sift into wet ingredients. Batter will be more thin. Flip soon while frying.

Buckwheat Granola
Nicole Hiebert

12 cups buckwheat sprouts* 4 tsp. cinnamon
1 cup coconut 3-4 cups chopped nuts
1 tsp. salt

Combine all the above in a large bowl. Place in a blender and whiz the following:

½ cup oil ½ cup pitted dates
½ cup honey ¼ cup flaxseeds
½ cup water

Pour into the large bowl and stir well. Either dehydrate at medium heat or bake in oven on low temperature until crispy. Store in refrigerator

*Buckwheat sprouts: Soak buckwheat for one day, then rinse and place in a colander with a plate underneath, rinsing 2 or 3 times a day for 2 or 3 days or until sprouts are about ¼" long.

For an all-time favorite breakfast at our house, we cook a pot of rice, and then we take a big scoop of rice and top it with honey, raisins, granola, cinnamon, sunflower seeds, yogurt, and milk.

Gluten-Free Grapenuts
Mrs Thomas Beachy

2½ cups buttermilk 1½ tsp. salt
2 tsp. soda 2 tsp. baking powder
1 Tbsp. vanilla 1 cup brown sugar
⅓ cup vegetable or olive oil 5 cups brown rice flour
½ tsp. stevia 1 cup tapioca flour
¼ tsp. xanthan gum

Mix all together. Bake in greased 9 x 13" pan for 45 minutes or until done. Allow cake to cool. Break into pieces and crumble by putting through a ¼" screen or use Salad Master. Put crumbs into pans and toast at 170° overnight or until dry. You don't need to stir if you don't put too thick a layer in the pan.

Granola

Mrs. Liana Cable

20 cups GF crispy rice cereal
5 tsp. cinnamon
1½ cup sesame seeds
1½ cup sunflower seeds
1 cup pumpkin seeds
2½ cups unsweetened coconut
2 cups carob chips (optional)

3 Tbsp. vanilla
¾ cup olive oil
2½ tsp. salt
2½ cups honey or maple syrup
2½ cups dried fruit

Mix all ingredients except fruit and carob chips. Spread into cake pans and bake 30-40 minutes at 300°. Stir every 10 minutes until toasted. Add dried fruit while granola is still warm, for it tends to cool in hard clumps that need to be broken apart. Serve with milk.

For a nutritious cereal breakfast in the morning, we boil millet which has been soaked overnight and add sweeteners (honey, raisins, bananas) and milk. Or we make cream of brown rice or cornmeal. One of my sisters enjoys filling her bowl with brown rice flakes and pouring boiling water over them to soak. Then she adds honey, fruit, cinnamon, and milk. Yummy!

—Nicole Hiebert

Gluten-Free
Main Dishes

Chicken Pot Pie

Mrs. Liana Cable

carrots   onions
potatoes   celery

Cook desired amount of vegetables in GF chicken broth or bouillon. Add peas after vegetables are cooked. Thicken with arrowroot powder or gluten-free flour. Place in a 9 x 13" baking dish and put batter on top.

Batter:

2 cups gluten-free flour   1 egg
2 tsp. baking powder   1 tsp. xanthan gum (optional)
1 cup dairy-free milk

Zucchini and Meat Quiche

Nicole Hiebert

Crust:

2 cups cooked brown rice   1 egg
½ cup grated cheese   ½ tsp. salt

Mix all four ingredients and pat into 9 x 13" pan. Bake at 350° for 8-10 minutes.

Filling:

3 cups grated zucchini   1 cup grated cheese
½ cup chopped onion   1 cup ground meat, cooked
2 Tbsp. butter   4 eggs
½ tsp. salt   1¼ cup milk
dash of pepper   ¼ tsp. white pepper (optional)

Saute zucchini, onion, salt, and pepper in butter until soft and moisture is all gone. Spread on rice crust. Sprinkle cheese over zucchini, then meat. Beat eggs and milk and pepper together. Pour over meat. Bake at 350° for 55-60 minutes, until puffed and golden. A knife should come out clean. Doubles well.

Rice, Corn, & Cheese Casserole Nicole Hiebert

3 cups cooked brown rice	½ tsp. salt
2 cups corn	½ tsp. chili powder
1 small onion	¼ tsp. pepper
2 cups grated cheddar	paprika
1½ cups milk	

Mix all ingredients well except paprika. Oil casserole dish lightly to avoid sticking. Pour into casserole dish, sprinkle with paprika. Bake 40-45 minutes at 350° (double time if you double recipe).

Gluten-Free Noodles Melinda Hollback

½ cup brown rice flour	1 tsp. gelatin powder
½ cup tapioca flour	½ tsp. salt
¼ cup potato starch	2 large eggs
½ cup cornstarch	¼ cup water
4 tsp. xanthan gum	

Mix together and cut out. Cuts better than flour noodles. I think they taste real close to the flour ones.

Beans and Dumplings Mrs. Joe Garber

1 Tbsp. olive oil	1 cup shredded carrots
1 onion	1 quart pinto beans
1 clove garlic	1 quart tomato juice
1 cup chopped celery	salt to taste

Saute first five ingredients till tender. Transfer all ingredients to a 4 quart roaster. Bring all to a boil. Top with biscuit dough, or Gluten-Free Bun dough (see page 38). Bake, covered, until biscuits are done.

Ezra's Favorite Beans

Susie Wiebe

Sort and rinse pinto beans (7 cups fill 5 quart slow cooker). Cover with water several inches deeper than the beans. Soak overnight. Drain and rinse well. Place in slow cooker. Add hot water to cover beans by a half inch or so. For each cup of beans add:

1 clove garlic, minced	1 bay leaf
½ tsp. coarse Celtic sea salt	

Simmer all day (about 8 hours). One hour before serving, remove and discard bay leaves. For each cup of dry beans, add:

½ tsp. paprika	½ tsp. cilantro (dry leaf)

Simmer for one more hour. These beans are so versatile. We like them with cooked brown rice and corn; warmed up tortilla shells spread with salsa and mashed avocado; mashed with salsa and avocado with corn chips for dipping; mixed into sloppy joes or chili; with fried eggs and corn bread, etc. I try to always have some of these canned beans in the fridge for quick meals or to take along. They are indispensable for gluten-free diets. To can beans, scoop hot beans into pint jars, seal, and heat in 200° oven for 20 minutes. Store in fridge. I use these beans when the recipe calls for canned beans, such as in Tamale Casserole.

Coconut Loaf

Mrs. Liana Cable

½ cup butter	2 tsp. baking powder
½ cup Sucanat	½ tsp. salt
2 eggs	¾ cup dairy-free milk
1 tsp. vanilla	1¼ cup coconut
2 cups gluten-free flour	

Cream butter and Sucanat. Add eggs and vanilla. Alternate dry ingredients with milk. Add coconut.

Tamale Casserole

Susie Wiebe

I found this recipe in the newspaper, made several changes to it, and it has become a favorite for our gluten-free son and his mom. Heat 1 Tbsp. butter in large saucepan over medium heat. Add:

1 medium onion, chopped	2 garlic cloves, squished

Cook, stirring, for about three minutes or until onion is softened. Add:

2 pints canned pinto beans	⅛ tsp. chili powder
½ tsp. oregano	½ tsp. fine Celtic sea salt

Bring to a boil, then add:

1 quart canned tomato pieces	1½ cups frozen corn kernels

Simmer, uncovered, stirring occasionally, for about 10 minutes. Transfer to 9 x 13" baking dish.

Topping: In a bowl, stir together:

¾ cup cornmeal	1 cup gluten-free flour
1 Tbsp. baking powder	

In another bowl, beat together:

1 egg	1 cup milk, sour cream, or water
1 Tbsp. melted honey	

Add liquid to flour mixture, stir briefly, then add:

2 Tbsp. melted butter

Stir till just combined. Spoon cornmeal batter over the bean mixture. Bake for 45 minutes at 350°. Serve with a green leafy salad or raw vegetables for a delicious, filling meal.

Gluten-Free Meatballs
Mrs. Elizabeth Beachy

2 lbs. hamburger
¼ cup water
2 eggs
½ cup chopped onions
½ tsp. garlic powder

2 tsp. salt (scant)
pepper
¼ tsp. chili powder (optional)
⅛ cup cornstarch
⅛ cup corn flour

In a bowl, mix water, eggs, and seasonings. Mix together cornstarch and corn flour. Stir into first mixture. Mix well. Add hamburger. Bake at 350° for one hour.

Sauce for meatballs:

2 cups ketchup
½ tsp. stevia powder
½ tsp. liquid smoke

1 tsp. garlic powder
¼ cup chopped onion
1 pepper, chopped

Make balls the size of walnuts, then pour sauce over them.

Best Ever Meatloaf
Lucia Lapp, Benton, IL

2 eggs
⅔ cup tomato juice
½ cup oatmeal
½ cup onion
½ cup grated carrot

1 cup mozzarella cheese (opt.)
1 tsp. parsley
1 tsp. salt
¼ tsp. pepper
1½ lb. hamburger

Topping:

½ cup tomato sauce   1 tsp. prepared mustard
¼ cup Sucanat

Bake at 350° for 45 minutes. Spoon topping on and bake another 30 minutes. Let stand 10 minutes before serving. Yield: 6 servings.

Homemade Noodles

Mrs. Rebecca Bontreger

2 dozen egg yolks
1 Tbsp. xanthan gum
½ cup water

2 tsp. salt
brown rice flour and
tapioca starch

Beat first four ingredients. For every cup of rice flour, add approximately ⅓ cup tapioca starch. Keep doing so till dough forms a ball. Do not add more flour than you have to. Put rice flour on counter and flour hands. Put small amounts out and roll with rolling pin. At this point you will be able to put them through noodle maker and get a desired thickness. Lay them on linens to dry some, flipping once to dry both sides. Keep checking for the correct dryness to put through the cutter. Put on linens again to dry completely, 2-3 days, before bagging them up. Very good noodles. Perhaps a couple more minutes are required to cook them soft. They warm up well. Cook them like regular noodles, with broth and seasoning.

GF Taco Shells

Mrs. Rebecca Bontreger

1 cup water
½ cup brown rice flour
½ cup tapioca starch
½ cup cornmeal

½ tsp. xanthan gum
¼ tsp. salt
1 egg

Batter must be quite thin. Fry in oiled skillet on both sides. Use shells to make warm roll-ups. Use your favorite toppings of sloppy joes, lettuce, tomatoes, Ranch dressing, cheese. Wrap up the toppings and eat while warm.

Deep Fat Fry Batter

Mrs. Rebecca Bontreger

1½ cup rice flour
½ cup tapioca starch
1 Tbsp. baking powder
1 Tbsp. paprika
2 Tbsp. sugar
1 tsp. garlic powder
1 tsp. onion powder
1 tsp. celery salt
water
1 egg yolk

Mix dry ingredients well. Add water till batter is thick and creamy. Last add yolk of egg. Cut chicken breast in crosswise narrow strips and put in batter. Stir till all the pieces are covered. Use fingers and pick out to put in prepared hot oil and deep fat fry till golden. Put in casserole dish, toweling lined, and keep in oven till all pieces are fried. Do not cover. Very delicious! Make stir-fry and use this for your meat. Add a sweet and sour sauce. Batter works for fish too.

Meat Breading

Mrs. Rebecca Bontreger

4 cups GF cornflakes
4 cups GF crispy rice cereal
2 cups rice flour
1 Tbsp. baking powder
1 Tbsp. garlic salt
2 Tbsp. paprika
3 Tbsp. Lawry's seasoning
2 Tbsp. onion powder
2 Tbsp. celery salt

Crush cornflakes and GF crispy rice cereal. Add flour and seasonings. Mix well. More salt and pepper may be added to suit your taste. Roll chicken in breading and fry in lard till golden. Put on sheets and bake till done. Can cover first half hour with wax paper laid over top without sealing off edges. Bake uncovered remaining time. Very crispy and tasty!

GF Brown Gravy
Mrs. Rebecca Bontreger

In skillet, melt 4 Tbsp. lard or use olive oil. Add your choice of seasonings, like celery salt, onion powder, garlic powder, soup base. Be sure to use some paprika. This makes it brown, but watch to avoid burning! Keep heat low. Add 2 Tbsp. rice flour and 2 Tbsp. clear jel. Brown a little again. Add chicken broth and water till it reaches your desired consistency. I also use this gravy to make stew by pouring it over steamed carrots, potatoes, onions, peas, etc. Delicious served over GF biscuits! (Page 46)

GF Pizza
Mrs. Rebecca Bontreger

Dough: Use GF "Wheat" Bread dough on page 25 or GF Biscuits dough on page 46 and press into black skillet pans. Sprinkle with garlic, cheese, and pizza seasonings. Add your choice of toppings. Bake dough before adding toppings.

Yeast-Free Pizza Crust
Vicky Selulluy

2 cups GF flour	1 Tbsp. dried basil
½ cup Parmesan cheese	4 Tbsp. butter
½ tsp. salt	5 Tbsp. olive oil
1 Tbsp. dried oregano	⅓ cup cold water

Preheat oven to 400°. Mix everything except the water together, then slowly add the water and knead as you add. Knead only for a few minutes till the dough is pliable. Form into a 6" disk and chill for 20 minutes in the refrigerator. Roll out onto a pizza pan and prick all over with a fork before adding your toppings. Bake for 20 minutes.

Jiffy Pizza Dough
Mrs. Thomas Beachy

2 cups rice flour
2 Tbsp. baking powder
1 tsp. salt

⅔ cup sour milk
⅓ cup olive oil

Mix everything together and press into large pan (11 x 17"). Top with browned hamburger and two cups GF pizza sauce. Let rise. Bake at 350° for 15-20 minutes, until dough is golden brown and crispy. Put cheese on top and let melt. Cut into portions and freeze the extra. This is very handy to thaw and heat for the gluten-intolerant person whenever our family has pizza.

Pizza Mix
Mrs. Liana Cable

2⅔ cups brown rice flour
2 cups tapioca flour
½ cup non-dairy milk powder
4 tsp. xanthan gum

2 tsp. salt
4 tsp. gelatin powder
4 tsp. Italian seasoning

Mix all together. For use in recipe below. Makes four 12" pizzas.

Pizza Crust
Mrs. Liana Cable

1⅓ cup pizza mix
1 Tbsp. dry yeast
⅔ cup warm water

¼ tsp. honey
1 tsp. olive oil
1 tsp. lemon juice

Mix with electric mixer on high speed. Press into a 12" pizza pan or a 9 x 13" baking dish.

Gluten-Free
Cakes &
Cupcakes

Carrot Cake
Nicole Hiebert

1 cup oil	1½ cup sugar
4 eggs	3 cups grated carrots
1 tsp. xanthan gum	2 cups GF Flour Mix*
2 tsp. baking soda	½ tsp. salt
2 tsp. cinnamon	¾ cup walnuts (optional)

Beat oil and sugar. Beat in eggs one at a time. Stir in carrots. Add rest of ingredients and stir to moisten. Put in greased 9 x 13" pan. Bake at 350° for 45 minutes or until toothpick comes out clean. Cool and frost. (Recipe for Cream Cheese Icing below.)
*See Nicole Hiebert's GF Flour Mix recipe on page 20.

Cream Cheese Icing
Nicole Hiebert

8 oz. cream cheese	¼ cup butter
4 cups GF icing sugar	2 tsp. vanilla

Beat slowly to mix and then beat until light and fluffy.

Apple Coffee Cake

Nicole Hiebert

Dry ingredients:

2⅔ cups GF Flour Mix*	½ tsp. salt
2½ tsp. xanthan gum	½ cup butter
6 tsp. baking powder	4 apples, peeled and sliced

Wet ingredients:

3 eggs, well-beaten	2 tsp. vanilla
1½ cup milk	¾ cup honey

Topping:

⅔ cup packed brown sugar	1 tsp. cinnamon

Combine GF Flour Mix, xanthan gum, baking powder, and salt in a large bowl. Cut or rub in butter until crumbly. Make a well in center. In another bowl, mix together WET ingredients. Pour into DRY. Stir well. Pour into greased 9 x 13" baking pan. Push apples well into batter. Mix topping and sprinkle over top. Bake in 350° oven for 50-60 minutes or until it begins to shrink from edge of pan. *See Nicole Hiebert's GF Flour Mix recipe on page 20.

Shoofly Cake

Donna Lois Wadel

4 cups brown rice flour	1½ cup brown sugar
¾ cup butter	

Mix thoroughly. Take out one cup crumbs and keep for top. To remaining crumbs add:

2 tsp. gelatin	2 tsp. xanthan gum

Mix thoroughly. Add:

1 cup molasses	2 cups boiling water
1 Tbsp. soda	1 or 2 beaten eggs

Mix well, then pour into greased 9 x 13" cake pan. Sprinkle remaining crumbs on top. Bake at 350° until done.

Gluten-Free Spice Cake

Melinda Hollback

1 cup brown rice flour
⅔ cup potato starch
⅓ cup tapioca starch
1 tsp. xanthan gum
1¾ tsp. baking soda
1 Tbsp. ground ginger
2 tsp. cinnamon
½ tsp. nutmeg

¼ tsp. cloves
1½ cup milk
1½ cup brown sugar
¼ cup butter, soft
¼ cup applesauce
⅓ cup molasses
2 eggs
1 Tbsp. vanilla

Preheat oven to 325°. Combine milk and brown sugar, bring to a boil. Remove from heat and add butter, applesauce, molasses, and vanilla. When butter melts add flours and remaining dry ingredients. Add eggs, mix well. Pour batter into greased pan. Bake 50 minutes or until toothpick inserted into center comes out clean.

Note: I have added nuts and raisins dusted in a little rice flour and baked in a tube pan drizzled with glaze.

Sweet Potato Cake
Nicole Hiebert

¼ cup butter	2 egg whites
1¼ cup GF Flour Mix*	¾ cup cooked and mashed yam
1 tsp. xanthan gum	8¾ oz. can undrained,
½ cup honey	crushed pineapple
2 tsp. cinnamon	1 tsp. vanilla
1 tsp. baking soda	1 cup chopped nuts
½ tsp. salt	

Melt butter in an 8" x 8" pan. Add remaining ingredients; mix with wooden spoon. Bake at 325° for 40-45 minutes. Doubling recipe can also make two small loaves of bread. *See Nicole Hiebert's GF Flour Mix recipe on page 20.

For a fast, scrumptious dessert, we buy a prepackaged White Cake mix from Celimix and pour the batter into a large rectangular glass pan, bake as directed, and cool, then make one package of instant vanilla pudding. Shortly before serving we spread the chilled pudding over the cake, top with whipped cream, and arrange strawberries on top! It isn't the healthiest dessert available, but once in a while is okay, right?

Angel Food Cake

Mrs. Rebecca Bontreger

1 cup white rice flour*   ¼ tsp. salt
½ cup tapioca starch   1 tsp. cream of tartar
1 cup white sugar   1 tsp. vanilla
2 cups egg whites

Sift flour, tapioca starch, and ½ cup white sugar together three times. Add salt, cream of tartar, and vanilla to egg whites and beat till stiff. Add remaining ½ cup sugar slowly and beat well. Gently fold in sifted flour with spoon. Bake at 350° till cake is browned and springs back when touched. Cool till cold, placed upside down. Cake may also be divided in two cake pans and used for delights.

*Must use white rice flour and not brown.

Banana Cake

Mrs. Esther Beachy

3 mashed bananas   ½ cup oil
3 eggs   1 cup sugar
1½ cup rice flour mix   ½ cup nuts
1 tsp. soda   1 tsp. vanilla
1 tsp. baking powder   ½ cup buttermilk or sour milk
1 tsp. salt   1 tsp. xanthan gum

Beat eggs and sugar until fluffy. Add oil and vanilla, mix till blended. Add sifted dry ingredients alternately with sour milk, mixing well after each addition. Add mashed bananas and nuts. Bake at 350° until done.

Gluten-Free Shortcake
Mrs. Thomas Beachy

2 eggs, well beaten	2½ tsp. baking powder
¼ cup olive oil	2 tsp. vanilla
⅛ cup honey or raw sugar	2 cups rice flour
1 cup sour milk or buttermilk	¼ tsp. stevia powder
½ tsp. baking soda	

Beat eggs hard until thick and fluffy. Add rest of ingredients without beating. Stevia may be mixed a bit into the flour before adding. When all the ingredients are added, stir well with a spoon. Pour into greased 9 x 13" pan. Bake at 400° for 20-25 minutes.

Lemon Pound Cake
Donna Lois Wadel

2¼ cups GF mix*	1¼ cup sugar
1⅛ tsp. xanthan gum	⅔ cup butter
1 tsp. egg replacer (optional)	½ cup milk
1 tsp. salt	1 Tbsp. lemon juice
1 Tbsp. grated lemon peel	3 eggs

Glaze: ½ cup sugar, ¼ cup lemon juice

Preheat oven to 325°. Grease a 9 x 5 x 3" loaf pan and dust with rice flour. In bowl of your mixer, place flour mix, xanthan gum, egg replacer, salt, sugar, and lemon peel. Make a well in the center and add milk and butter. Stir to combine. Scrape bowl, turn to low speed, and beat one minute. Add lemon juice and eggs. Beat on low for about 30 seconds. Scrape bowl down again. Turn to medium speed and beat one minute or until fluffy. Spoon batter in prepared pan and bake for one hour and 10 minutes. Cool in pan a few minutes before turning out. Glaze while still hot. For glaze: In a saucepan, heat sugar and lemon juice to boiling. Brush on cake while still warm. The cake should absorb all the glaze. 12-16 servings. *See Donna Lois Wadel's GF Mix recipe on page 21.

Chocolate Zucchini Cupcakes

Nicole Hiebert

½ cup sour milk*
½ cup oil
3 eggs
2½ cups GF Flour Mix*
4 Tbsp. cocoa
1 tsp. salt
1 tsp. vanilla

½ cup butter
1¾ cup sugar
2 cups grated, peeled zucchini
1¼ tsp. xanthan gum
½ tsp. baking powder
1 tsp. baking soda
½-⅔ cup chocolate chips

Put everything in bowl except chocolate chips and beat on high for 4 minutes. Stir in chips and scoop into cupcake papers or oiled muffin tins. Bake for 15-20 minutes at 350°. *Sour milk—add 1½ tsp. vinegar to regular milk. *See Nicole Hiebert's GF Flour Mix recipe on page 20.

Apple Cupcakes

Mrs. Thomas Beachy

½ cup raw sugar
¾ cup oil
1 large egg
2 tsp. baking powder
½ tsp. soda

½ tsp. salt
½ tsp. vanilla
1¼ cups rice flour
1½ cups chopped pecans
1½ cups chopped apples

Beat together sugar, oil, and egg. Add remaining ingredients. Mix well. Bake at 350° for 25 minutes.

Banana Cupcakes

Mrs. Thomas Beachy

3 bananas, or 1½ cup
3 cups rice flour
1½ tsp. baking powder
¾ tsp. baking soda
¾ tsp. salt
¾ cup olive oil

2¼ cups raw sugar
1½ tsp. vanilla
3 eggs
6 Tbsp. sour milk
¾ cup pecans

Beat olive oil and eggs. Add sugar, vanilla, and milk. Add bananas with dry ingredients. Add ¾ cup chopped pecans or ground nuts. Bake at 375° for 15 minutes.

my gluten-free notes

_____
_____
_____
_____
_____
_____
_____
_____
_____
_____
_____
_____
_____
_____
_____
_____
_____
_____
_____
_____
_____

Gluten-Free
Cookies

Wheat-Free Cookies
Mrs. Joe Garber

3 cups gluten-free flour mix ¾ tsp. salt
¾ cup tapioca flour 1 cup shredded unsweetened
2 cups oatmeal coconut
1 Tbsp. baking powder 1 cup butter or coconut oil

Mix well. In a separate bowl, mix the following:

½ cup applesauce ½ cup orange juice
½ cup maple syrup concentrate
1 cup chocolate chips 1 tsp. vanilla

Combine ingredients of both bowls. Chill dough, form balls, flatten before baking. Bake at 375° until browned.

Gluten-Free Cookies
Mrs. Liana Cable

1¼ cup butter or olive oil 5 tsp. xanthan gum
2 cups Sucanat 1 tsp. salt
5 cups gluten-free flour 3 Tbsp. vanilla
2½ cups pecan meal nuts, chocolate chips, raisins,
5 eggs* sunflower seeds or your choice
2½ tsp. baking soda

Beat butter and Sucanat. Mix flour and other dry ingredients. Add to butter mixture. Beat well. Add eggs. Then add your choice of extras. This is a stiff dough. Bake at 350° for 15 minutes. *You can substitute 5 tsp. flaxseed meal dissolved in 1¼ cup hot water.

Tapioca Honey Cookies
Mrs. Elizabeth Beachy

¾ cup lard*
⅔ cup honey
1 large egg
1½ cup tapioca flour
2½ cups rice flour

½ tsp. cinnamon
1 tsp. vanilla
1 tsp. baking powder
1 ripe banana

Mix like regular cookies. Bake at 350°. For variation, add chocolate chips, or for sorghum cookies, substitute honey with sorghum and add ½ tsp. ginger. *Original recipe called for 1 cup margarine; lard may be reduced.

Chocolate Chip Cookies
Serena Yoder

¾ cup brown rice flour
½ cup tapioca flour
¼ cup potato starch flour
1 tsp. baking soda
½ tsp. xanthan gum
¼ tsp. salt (optional)

¼ cup butter or substitute
¾ cup raw sugar
2 tsp. vanilla
1 extra large egg
1 cup chocolate chips
¼ cup chopped nuts (optional)

Mix flours, baking soda, xanthan gum and salt in small bowl. In a large mixing bowl, beat butter, sugar, vanilla and egg. Beat in flour mixture on low speed; mix well. Stir in chocolate chips and nuts. Drop by tablespoonful onto greased cookie sheet. Press them down to ½ inch thickness if desired. Bake 10-12 minutes (or until lightly browned) at 350° on center rack of oven. Cool 2-3 minutes before removing from cookie sheet. Makes 24 cookies.

Peanut Butter Cookies
Serena Yoder

1 cup applesauce
¼ cup canola oil
1 mashed banana
1 cup GF peanut butter
1 cup brown sugar*
1½-2 cups rice flour

1 cup tapioca flour
½ cup potato starch flour
2 Tbsp. water*
2 tsp. baking soda
6 Tbsp. cornstarch

Place applesauce, oil and banana in large mixing bowl. Mix till smooth. Add peanut butter, brown sugar and water. Mix flours, baking soda and cornstarch. Add to liquid mixture. Mix well. Batter will be runny. Drop by rounded teaspoonfuls or cookie scoop. Dip fork in water and flatten cookies to ½ inch thickness. Bake at 325° for 12-15 minutes. Centers should be slightly soft. When they cool they are harder, so underbake for a softer cookie. You may substitute ½-1 cup honey for brown sugar. *Omit water if using honey.

Chocolate Chip Cookies
Patricia Taylor

¾ cup rice flour
½ cup tapioca flour
¼ cup potato starch

½ tsp. baking soda
1 tsp. xanthan gum
¼ tsp. salt

Mix above together. Add:

¼ cup shortening
¾ cup brown sugar
1 large egg
5 Tbsp. sugar

2 tsp. vanilla
1 cup chocolate chips
¼ cup walnuts

Put in 8 x 8" pan for 25-30 minutes at 350°. Or makes 24 cookies. Flatten with glass. Bake 10-12 minutes.

Soft Raisin Cookies
Mrs. Thomas Beachy

1 cup water	1 tsp. baking powder
2 cups raisins	1 tsp. baking soda
1 cup soft butter	1 tsp. salt
1¾ cups raw sugar	½ tsp. cinnamon
2 eggs, lightly beaten	½ tsp. nutmeg
1 tsp. vanilla	½ cup chopped walnuts
3½ cups rice flour	

Combine raisins and water in a small saucepan; bring to boil. Cook for three minutes; remove from heat and let cool (do not drain). In a mixing bowl cream butter; gradually add sugar. Add eggs and vanilla. Combine dry ingredients; gradually add to creamed mixture and blend thoroughly. Stir in nuts and raisins. Drop by teaspoonfuls 2" apart on greased baking sheets. Bake at 350° for 12-14 minutes. Yield: about 6 dozen. These are delicious!

Chocolate Chip Cookies
Mrs. Rebecca Bontreger

½ cup brown sugar	1½ cup brown rice flour
½ cup white sugar	½ cup tapioca starch
⅔ cup olive oil	2 tsp. soda
3 eggs, well beaten	1 tsp. baking powder
1 Tbsp. vanilla	2 Tbsp. Dari-Free*
1 tsp. salt	1 tsp. xanthan gum

Mix wet ingredients. Add dry ingredients from sifter. Mix well. Add ⅓ cup chocolate chips and nuts optionally. Bake at 375°. *Dari-Free is available at Vance's Foods, 1.800.497.4834.

Sorghum Pumpkin Cookies Mrs. Rebecca Bontreger

3 eggs, well beaten
¾ cup olive oil
½ cup white sugar
½ cup brown sugar
½ cup squash or pumpkin
½ cup sorghum
1 tsp. salt
1 Tbsp. soda

2 tsp. baking powder
1 tsp. cloves
2 tsp. cinnamon
2 tsp. ginger
1 Tbsp. xanthan gum
1⅓-1½ cup brown rice flour
½ cup tapioca starch
nuts (optional)

Beat eggs well. Add all the rest of ingredients except starch, flour and xanthan gum. Sift these ingredients in. Beat well till dough stiffens up. Drop by teaspoonfuls. Bake at 375°. Cookies are very soft and moist. Will stay soft till they're all eaten! Do not overbake.

Gingersnaps Ina Schrock

¾ cup molasses
6 Tbsp. coconut oil
1½ cup rice flour
1 cup pumpkin seed meal*

2 tsp. ginger
½ tsp. soda
¼ tsp. red pepper (optional)

Bring the molasses and coconut oil to a boil. Cool. Combine remaining ingredients and add to the liquid ingredients. Refrigerate. When chilled, form into a 2" round log. Freeze. Then slice frozen dough into ¼" slices and bake for 10 minutes at 350°. Transfer to wire racks to cool. They will get crisp as they cool. Makes 4 dozen. *Pumpkin seeds ground in a coffee grinder.

Gingersnaps
Laura Miller

¾ cup vegetable shortening ½ tsp. xanthan gum
1 cup granulated sugar 1 tsp. cinnamon
1 large egg ¾ tsp. ground ginger
¼ cup molasses ¼ tsp. ground cloves
1¾ cup Brown Rice Flour Mix* ¼ tsp. salt
¼ cup sweet rice flour granulated sugar
2 tsp. baking soda

Beat shortening and sugar in large bowl of electric mixer until light and creamy. Beat in egg and molasses and mix until smooth. Add flours, baking soda, xanthan gum, cinnamon, ginger, cloves and salt; mix to form a soft dough. Refrigerate for 30 minutes. Preheat oven to 350°. Position rack in center of oven. Lightly grease cookie sheet with cooking spray. Use your hands to shape dough into 1" balls. Roll balls in sugar and place on cookie sheet. Bake 8-10 minutes or until baked through. Transfer to wire rack and cool. Store in airtight container. *Brown Rice Flour Mix: 6 cups brown rice flour, 2 cups potato starch, 1 cup tapioca flour. Mix well. Total: 9 cups.

Gluten-Free Brownies
Mrs. Rebecca Bontreger

Melt in saucepan:
  ½ cup shortening
Stir in:
  ½ cup cocoa 1 cup white sugar
Take off heat. Add:
  2 eggs, beaten well ¾ cup rice flour
  1 tsp. vanilla 2 tsp. baking powder
  ¼ tsp. salt ½ cup nuts
Bake at 350-375° for 15-20 minutes. Yummy!

GF Pumpkin Bars

Mrs. Rebecca Bontreger

4 eggs, well beaten	1½ cups brown rice flour
⅔ cup olive oil	½ cup tapioca starch
1½ cup white sugar	2 tsp. xanthan gum
1½ cup pumpkin or squash	1 Tbsp. baking powder
2 tsp. vanilla	1 tsp. soda
1 tsp. salt	2 tsp. cinnamon

Mix wet ingredients. Sift dry ingredients in. Mix well and pour on cookie sheet. Bake at 375° till touch springs back. Make frosting with 4 oz. cream cheese and 1 cup Rich's topping, whipped and mixed together. Sprinkle ground nuts over top. Very moist and tasty!

GF Coffee Bars

Mrs. Rebecca Bontreger

2 cups brown sugar	½ cup tapioca starch
1 cup prepared rich coffee	2 tsp. soda
⅔ cup olive oil	1 tsp. baking powder
2 tsp. vanilla	1 tsp. salt
3 eggs, well beaten	1 Tbsp. xanthan gum
1½ cups brown rice flour	

Mix first five ingredients. Sift dry ingredients in. Mix well. Pour on large cookie sheet and sprinkle chocolate chips and nuts on top. Bake at 375° till touch springs back. Delicious!

Gluten-Free
Desserts

Rice Pie Crust
Mrs. Elvin Zimmerman

1½ cup butter	2 Tbsp. water
3 cups brown rice flour	2 eggs

Mix all ingredients together well. Roll between waxed paper or plastic wrap and fit into two pie plates or one two-crust pie. Bake at 350° for 8-10 minutes, unfilled. Either prebake slightly if using filling or bake at 425° for 10 minutes, on lowest shelf, then reduce to 350° for 10 or more minutes until done.

Apple Pie Filling
Mrs. Elvin Zimmerman

5 cups apples, sliced	½ cup raisins (optional)
1½ cup apple juice	⅛ tsp. cinnamon
3 Tbsp. tapioca or cornstarch	¼ tsp. salt

Soak tapioca in apple juice while peeling apples. Combine ingredients and bring to a boil. Pour into two 9" Rice Pie Crusts.

Streusel Topping
Mrs. Elvin Zimmerman

1 cup + 2 Tbsp. brown rice flour	⅛ tsp cloves
¾ cup ground almonds	3 Tbsp. oil
¼ tsp. cinnamon	3 Tbsp. honey

Mix dry ingredients. Drizzle oil and honey over top and mix until evenly mixed together. Put on top of two pies. Also can be used in fruit crisps, one 9 x 13" pan or two 8" pans. Sprinkle crumbs over tops for the last 15 minutes of baking time so they don't over brown. Unbaked crumbs may be frozen for later use.

Pecan Pie
Mrs. Liana Cable

1 gluten-free pie crust*
¾ cup maple syrup
½ cup Sucanat
3 eggs, slightly beaten

⅓ cup melted butter
½ tsp. salt
1 tsp. vanilla
1½ cup chopped pecans

In mixing bowl, combine maple syrup, Sucanat, eggs, butter, salt and vanilla, mix well. Pour filling into unbaked pie shell. Sprinkle with pecan pieces. Bake at 350° for 50 minutes. *See following recipe.

GF Pie Crust
Mrs. Liana Cable

1¼ cup brown rice flour
1 cup tapioca flour
½ tsp. baking soda
½ tsp. xanthan gum

½ tsp. salt
½ cup olive oil
¼ cup butter
¼ cup milk

Mix dry ingredients together. Add oil and butter. Mix until crumbly like cornmeal. Add milk. Mix very well. Press into a pie pan and crimp edges. I usually get two pie crusts from this recipe unless I want a thick crust.

Baby Pecan Pies

Laura Miller

Pastry Shells:

3 oz. cream cheese, softened	½ cup butter, softened
½ cup rice flour	½ cup potato starch

Combine cream cheese and butter in a small bowl, stir till smooth. Mix rice flour and potato starch. Add to first mixture, mixing well. Chill dough one hour. Shape into 24 1" balls. Place in ungreased muffin tins, shaping each into a shell.

Filling:

¾ cup packed brown sugar	1 Tbsp. butter
1 egg	dash of salt
1 tsp. vanilla	¾ cup chopped pecans

Combine first five ingredients in a small bowl; beat at medium speed till smooth.

Layer the following ingredients in a pastry shell:

½ tsp. pecans	½ tsp. pecans
1 tsp. filling	

Bake at 325° for 20-25 minutes. Freezes well.

Non-Gluten Pie Crust

Serena Yoder

1¼ cup brown rice flour
1 cup tapioca flour
1 Tbsp. raw sugar
½ tsp. baking soda

2 tsp. xanthan gum
½ tsp. salt (optional)
¾ cup butter substitute
¼ cup milk

Place dry ingredients in medium mixing bowl. Mix well. Add butter substitute and mix till texture of bread crumbs. Add milk and mix well. If it looks too dry add a little more milk—1 Tbsp. at a time, till you can make a nice ball. Can chill dough one hour if it is too soft to handle. Roll half of dough between two pieces of plastic wrap (tape bottom piece to countertop so it doesn't slide around). To place in 8" pie pan, remove top piece of plastic wrap and place pan upside down onto dough, then lift up the taped corners of the bottom piece and tape to the bottom of pan. Carefully put hand under dough and put other hand on pie pan and flip it over. Remove plastic wrap and push any cracks together. Fill with filling of choice. Roll out remaining dough between plastic wrap. Carefully flip it onto your filled pie crust or put into another pie pan for pies with no top crust. Push and pinch dough to form ridge around rim of pie plate. Watch pie carefully to avoid burning. May need to lower oven temperature 10° in order not to burn crust.

Tender Vinegar Pastry

Patricia Taylor

1½ cup rice flour	1 tsp. xanthan gum
½ cup potato starch flour	¾ cup shortening
¼ cup tapioca flour	1 egg, lightly beaten
1 tsp. salt	2 Tbsp. apple cider vinegar
1 Tbsp. sugar	2 Tbsp. cold water

Sift the flours, salt, sugar and xanthan gum into mixing bowl. Cut in the shortening. Blend together the beaten egg, vinegar and cold water. Stir them into the flour mix. This will seem quite moist, but a rice crust needs to be more moist than wheat. Knead into a ball (dough won't toughen). Separate into two balls and roll between two sheets of plastic wrap. To place into pie tin, remove top sheet, invert dough and lay into the pan. Prebake the crust in 450° oven for 10-12 minutes. Fill pie crust and follow directions for pie.

Jelly Roll

Nicole Hiebert

¾ cup white sugar	¾ cup potato starch flour
4 eggs	1 tsp. baking powder
1 tsp. vanilla	¼ tsp. salt

Beat eggs and sugar in top of double boiler until lukewarm. Remove from heat and beat until thick and creamy (use electric mixer). Add vanilla. Gradually add potato starch flour with salt and baking powder. Pour into large, shallow pan (11 x 15"), lined with greased waxed paper. Bake at 350° for 20-25 minutes, or until it looks done. Remove from pan, placing it on a cloth sprinkled with gluten-free icing sugar. Take off paper. Trim off edges. Spread with jelly (which has been beaten with a fork) or prepared cooked pie filling. Roll up quickly and wrap in towel until cake cools. You do have to work fast or cake will crack as it cools.

For a really weak moment. Yummy, yummy!

Blackberry Cobbler
Mrs. Thomas Beachy

1 quart canned wild blackberries

Drain juice; add enough water to make four cups of juice. Add:

¼ cup raw sugar	¼ tsp. stevia
½ cup Perma-Flo	

Bring to boil, stirring constantly. When thickened, stir in blackberries. Pour filling into 9 x 13" pan. Top with shortcake batter. Bake at 350° for 40-45 minutes.

Blueberry Buckle
Mrs. Thomas Beachy

1 egg, well beaten	4 tsp. baking powder
¼ cup olive oil	¼ tsp. salt
⅛ cup raw sugar or honey	½ tsp. stevia
1 cup sour milk	2 cups frozen, unsweetened
2 cups rice flour	blueberries

Topping: (optional)

½ cup rice flour	¼ cup soft butter
¼ cup raw sugar	½ tsp. cinnamon
	(if using apples)

Mix egg, oil, and honey thoroughly. Add rest of ingredients except blueberries and mix well. Add blueberries and mix gently. Spread into a greased 9 x 13" pan. Mix topping, if desired, and sprinkle on top of batter. Bake at 375° for 45-50 minutes. Serve warm with milk. Apples may be used instead of blueberries. Canned, well-drained blueberries may also be used instead of frozen. This is a family favorite!

GF Doughnut Balls

Mrs. Rebecca Bontreger

1½ cup brown rice flour
½ cup tapioca starch
½ cup potato starch (opt.)
⅔ cup brown sugar
1 Tbsp. baking powder
1 tsp. salt
¼ tsp. nutmeg

¼ tsp. cinnamon
2 beaten eggs
½ cup rice milk
1 Tbsp. olive oil
2 tsp. vanilla
½ cup powdered sugar
2 tsp. cinnamon

Sift dry ingredients into bowl. Mix wet ingredients. Mix together and beat well with spoon. Dough will be barely stiff enough to manage. Dip fingers into tapioca starch and form tiny quarter-size balls. Have oil heated. Test try some. Do not have oil too hot. Make a favorite glaze and dip into powdered sugar and cinnamon. These taste like cake doughnuts from the store. Very good! Yummy while fresh.

Fresh Apple Salad

Mrs. Elizabeth Beachy

Sauce:

1 beaten egg
½ cup honey
⅛ tsp. stevia (optional)
1 pint water

2 Tbsp. vinegar
1 Tbsp. butter
vanilla
3 Tbsp. cornstarch

Heat honey, water and vinegar. Thicken with cornstarch. Beat egg, quickly whisk 1 cup of hot mixture into beaten egg and return to saucepan. Let come to a slight boil. Remove from heat and add butter and vanilla. Cool, then add:

6 diced apples
½ cup celery, diced fine
½ cup nuts

sliced bananas
pineapple
diced cheese

You may want to add dried fruit—raisins, dates, etc. Note: The original recipe asked for 2 Tbsp. flour. For those who are allergic to eggs and dairy, you may wish to omit the egg, butter and cheese.

Gelatin Ice Cream

Mrs. Elizabeth Beachy

2 quarts milk	¾ cup water
½ cup honey	2 eggs
¼ tsp. stevia powder	1 cup cream
2 Tbsp. gelatin, soaked	2 tsp. vanilla

Heat one quart of milk and honey in a kettle till hot but not boiling. Soak gelatin in water till dissolved; add to hot milk. Cool till jelled. Beat cream and eggs; add this and one quart raw milk to mixture; add vanilla. Pour into ice cream freezer and freeze. Yield: 1 gallon. I omit the cream, as we use goat's milk. The yield may be less. Variation: Black Cherry Ice Cream: Put in one extra tablespoon of gelatin to recipe. When almost done add two cups slightly chopped and pitted sweet cherries and also cherry juice. Add ½ tsp. almond flavoring; omit vanilla. Strawberry Ice Cream: Follow directions as for Black Cherry Ice Cream except put in 2-3 cups of mashed strawberries. You may add the almond flavoring if desired.

my gluten-free notes

Gluten-Free

Miscellaneous

Nut Butter
Serena Yoder

4 cups almonds
4 cups cashews
4 cups pecan meal or pecans
3 cups olive oil

Put through juicer to make nut butter. May need to add more oil if too dry.

Homemade French Dressing
Susie Wiebe

Place in quart jar:

1 cup extra virgin olive oil
1 cup homemade ketchup
½ cup honey
¼ cup apple cider vinegar
½ tsp. onion powder
1 tsp. dry mustard*

Shake well. Delicious over mixed greens. We even like it over coleslaw and sprouts in place of coleslaw dressing. *May be substituted with 1 Tbsp. prepared mustard.

Crackers
Mrs. Larry (Liana) Cable

6 cups gluten-free flour
2 cups pecan meal
¾ cup butter
1 tsp. salt
2 tsp. baking powder
2 tsp. xanthan gum

Mix and add enough milk to make a soft dough. Roll out on cookie sheet to desired thickness. Cut into squares with a pizza cutter. Bake at 375° for 20 minutes or until desired crispiness is reached.

Index

Biscuits

Breakfast

Cakes and Cupcakes

Cookies

Desserts

Flour Mixes

Main Dishes

Misc.

Muffins

Quick Breads

Yeast Breads

Eat Healthy Food — Be Healthy!

Healthy Choices

- No Sugar
- No White Flour
- No Artificial Anything
- 1093 Recipes
- 26 Categories

· *7" x 10". 464 pages · spiral bound*
· *1,093 recipes · laminated cover*

Healthy Choices ... Item #126 ... **$15.99**

- **Recipes for Familiar Food**
  - · Breads
  - · Meats
  - · Desserts
  - · Canning

- **Recipes for Special Tastes**
  - · Meat Substitutes
  - · Lacto-Fermented
  - · Dairy
  - · Sourdough
  - · Cooking With Herbs

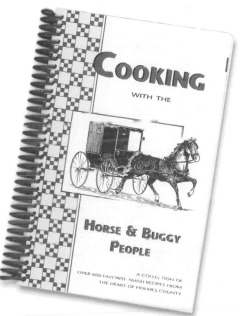

VOLUME II

Cooking with the Horse & Buggy People

Sharing a Second Serving of Favorites
from 207 Amish Women of Holmes County, Ohio

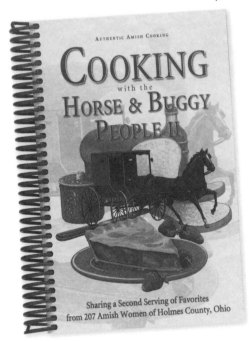

Henry and Amanda Mast, authors and compilers of *Cooking with the Horse and Buggy People Volume II* (as well as Volume I), live close to Charm, Ohio. Their home place is in the heart of the world's largest Amish community. The Masts and their friends worked countless hours in the kitchen to perfect the 600 recipes they chose to share with you.

Good food. Laughter. Compliments. Memories. That's what this new volume of *Cooking with the Horse and Buggy People* is about.

· 5¹/₂" x 8¹/₂" · 320 pp · Spiral Bound · Extra-Heavy Laminated Cover

Cooking with the Horse & Buggy People ... Item #628 ... **$12.99**

Give Us This Day Our Daily Bread

All the favorites of the Belle Center Amish Community. Over 600 of today's family favorites and even some from Grandma's kitchen. All the usual sections are here. But what makes this one special is the appetizers, large quantity recipes (for weddings, reunions, and other special occasions) and the children's recipe section. The tips, hints, and quotes section is filled with everyday kitchen secrets.

· $5^1/_2$" x $8^1/_2$" · 263 pp · Spiral bound · Indexed

Give Us This Day Our Daily Bread … Item #733 … **$11.99**

AUTHENTIC AMISH COOKING

The Wooden Spoon
Cookbook

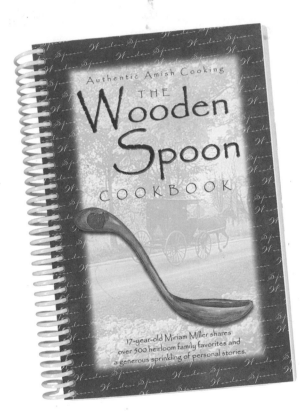

Meet 17-year-old Miriam Miller in the *Wooden Spoon Cookbook*. In addition to sharing her own, her mother's, and her grandmother's favorite recipes, Miriam shares childhood memories, stories, and personal details of her life as a young Amish girl.

· 5¹/₂" x 8¹/₂" · 194 pp · Spiral bound · Laminated cover · Double indexed

The Wooden Spoon Cookbook … Item #415 … **$10.99**